Natural Evangelism

Sharing the Gospel in Ways that are Truly Good

Leader's Guide

Dwight Marable

TCN
TRANSFORMING
CHURCHES
NETWORK

For more information, please contact
Transforming Churches Network
1160 Vickery Ln. Ste #1, Cordova, TN 38016
901-757-9700
www.tcnprocess.com
terry@transformingchurchesnetwork.org

Table of Contents

Introduction   5

1. The Faith Journey   9

2. Improving Your Serve   15

3. Improve Your Serve Together   21

4. Friendship through Listening   27

5. Friendship through Curiosity   33

6. Natural Sharing   39

Introduction

Through the years, Christians commonly confess that sharing the Gospel of Jesus Christ with those who don't know Jesus feels like an ominous, daunting task. Even though they have experienced the good news of Jesus Christ as good news and they are glad that they are Christians, sharing the good news with others feels unnatural, as if they are trying to force something that is less than good upon people.

The New Testament word Gospel means "good news." It's the word used when a messenger traveled home from the battlefront to deliver the news of victory at war. He announced the good news. He announced the gospel. As a messenger, he was a witness of victory that others could not see and had not experienced. Through this witness, others were included in on the victory.

In the Old Testament, the same kind of imagery shaped the meaning. For instance, the prophet Isaiah wrote:

> You who bring good news to Zion, go up on a high mountain. You who bring good news to Jerusalem, lift up your voice with a shout, lift it up, do not be afraid; say to the towns of Judah, "Here is your God!" —Isaiah 40:9

Our word "evangelism" is a derivative of the Greek word we translate Gospel. It's kinda weird that this is not obvious in the English language, but literally it could mean something like "good newsing." If the good news is really good, then shouldn't there be ways of sharing this good news that are also good?

This is what the six sessions of *Natural Evangelism* are all about. As you walk through these discussions and exercises as a group, you will discover natural ways to share the good news that demonstrates that both the message and the method is actually good. How we share the Gospel is just as important as what we share.

Here's the good news for you: By learning how to share the Gospel through these sessions, you will discover ways of sharing that tear down walls between you and non-Christians while also learning how to point them to the truth of Jesus.

Ways To Use This Resource

The six sessions found in this study guide can be used in various settings. They include the following:

• Small group that meets in a home. These studies work very well for groups.

• In an adult Sunday school class or Bible study. These can be done in small and large classes. If your class has more than 20 members, break members into small groups for the activities that require discussion.

• As a church-wide campaign emphasis. These six sessions can be studied as part of a church-wide program. The pastor can preach six sermons that correlate with the six sessions. And various groups can be organized, whether small groups that meet in homes or Sunday school classes that meet on the church campus. For a complete guide on how to organize such an effort, download the Church-wide Campaign Guide which can be found on the Transforming Churches Network website (www.tcnprocess.com).

Supplies Needed for These Studies

General Supplies
- ❑ DVD Player or VCR
- ❑ TV
- ❑ Leader's Guide
- ❑ Participant's Guides
- ❑ Legal Pad
- ❑ Markers

Session 1: The Faith Journey
- ❑ Legal Pad
- ❑ Markers/Crayons

Session 2: Improving Your Serve
- ❑ Bibles

Session 3: Improving Your Serve (Together!)
- ❑ Sister Act DVD or VHS - view clip at 58:28-1:03:15
- ❑ DVD Player or VCR
- ❑ Bibles

Session 4: Friendship through Listening
- ❑ Whiteboard/Flipchart Paper/Markers
- ❑ Four or Five Simple Pictures from a Magazine
- ❑ Pens

Session 5: Friendship through Curiosity
- ❑ Bibles
- ❑ Legal Pad
- ❑ Candy for Prizes

Session 6: Natural Sharing
- ❑ Pens

Session 1

The Faith Journey

Objective: *People who don't know Jesus are at different places on their faith journeys. In this session, we will discover how to understand where different people are on the journey and how to relate to them best.*

Discovery Activity

Planting a New Lawn

Facilitator Instructions: This is a partnership activity where you will group everyone in pairs. Feel free to get people paired up with folks they wouldn't necessarily sit next to. Hand each group a couple of pieces of white paper (or poster board/flip chart paper) and some crayons or markers. Give these instructions to each pair: "You have 5 minutes to draw your best picture of what it takes to plant a new lawn. Think of the various steps involved in planting a new lawn and include them in your picture. Ready…Go!"

Debrief

After 5 minutes are up, ask each pair to share their drawings with everyone else by briefly explaining what they have depicted. Next, lead a brief discussion of group reflection with the following questions:

Question #1: To recap, what are the steps involved in planting a new lawn?

Question #2: In what ways is the process of planting a new lawn like the process of someone coming to faith in Christ? (Allow the group to make as many connections as possible, particularly around the word "process.")

Learning Activity

Give everyone a few minutes to read the following article on understanding the various stages of a person coming to faith in Christ. After everyone has read it, ask a few open-ended questions to encourage people to interact with the information.

Understanding Faith Stages

In a very helpful book entitled *Irresistible Evangelism*, authors Sjogren, Ping, and Pollock liken the faith stages of an individual to playing golf. When you consider an average hole on a golf course, often the hole is some 400 yards away from where you first strike the ball in the tee area. The reality for most of us is that it will take quite a few swings to get the ball down to where the flag is on the putting green. One hit will not get us there. We must work our way down the fairway through a number of skillful shots.

One of the other peculiarities of golf is that there are a number of different clubs. Each club has a special purpose and needs to be used at the right occasion. Choosing the right club relates to where you are on the course and how far away your ball is from the putting green. Now, how does this all relate to faith stages? Coming to faith in Christ is a process just like moving a ball down a fairway.

People in the Tee Box:
People in the tee box are way back at the beginning of the hole. When they think of God, it's a pretty random thought. These folks have a long way to go before they get on to the putting green. What will help move someone who is on the tee box and is far from God? The authors in *Irresistible Evangelism* suggest that acts of kindness from Christians are sure-fire ways to help move someone down the fairway. Performing loving acts of service is the best "club" to use with someone who hasn't even hit the ball yet.

> It often takes many unexpected acts of generosity in Christ's name to soften their hostile stances and help them move toward a more neutral place. Servant evangelism "moves the ball" great distances by meeting simple needs with such actions as quenching a person's thirst or washing a person's car for free. No strings attached thoughtfulness gently counters negative perceptions…Genuine acts of kindness work no matter where people are in relationship to God, so they are always a great way to start the ball rolling (81).

People in the Fairway:
Folks in the fairway are distracted by a number of things. Their ball could be stuck in the trees or stuck in a sand trap. They are probably moving through life at warp speed and are balancing home, hobbies, and work pressures. God, in all likelihood, is squeezed out of their lives. Sjogren, Ping, and Pollock suggest:

> To connect with folks in this place requires genuine friendliness. Irresistible evangelists give friends practical support, meeting their emotional needs by providing a listening ear and a non-judgmental shoulder to lean on—and perhaps cry on. As trust in a Christian friend increases, a person's openness to spiritual subjects will usually grow (81).

People Approaching the Green:
At some point an individual may begin to start pondering their position in life. It may start with a gnawing sense of doubt, or a catalytic event could push them toward evaluating significant issues like purpose and destiny. We can help move this person closer to the green by "asking sensitive, 'active wondering' questions that stretch their thinking and open up new perspectives. If we have listened well and have prepared the way with true friendship, people will often start actively seeking God and asking lots of questions" (81).

Getting the Ball in the Hole:
Once a person has navigated down the fairway, it's a short putt to get the "spiritual ball" to drop into the hole. Ultimately, this is the job of the Holy Spirit. We have simply been God's instrument to help nudge the person closer to God's saving work.

Debrief

Question #1: Place someone that you know on the golf course and tell us where they are in relation to God. What do you think it would take to get that person's "spiritual ball" moving closer to the hole?

Question #2: What are some examples from the New Testament of:

- a person in the tee box
- a person in the fairway
- a person approaching the green
- putting the ball in the hole

Question #3: What are you intrigued by or personally challenged by as you read through this article?

Question #4: What are some of the unique challenges Christians face in sharing God's love with someone who is:

- in the tee box
- in the fairway
- approaching the putting green
- ready to putt for the hole

10 minutes

Application Activity

Getting In Some Practice

Facilitator Instructions: In groups of three, brainstorm a variety of ways that Christians could reach out to non-Christians using the golf illustration. Be creative with the kinds of actions, questions, and approaches you think would be appropriate for a non-Christian depending on where they are on the course.

In the Tee Box

In the Fairway

Approaching the Green

On the Putting Green

Application Activity

10
minutes

Golfers in My World

Facilitator Instructions: On your own, think of at least five people you know who need the love of God in their lives (friends, neighbors, co-workers, family members, etc.). Estimate where they are on the "spiritual golf course." In the last column, jot down specific steps you could take to help them move their "spiritual ball."

Name	Position on the Course	Actions I Could Take

10
minutes

Wrap-Up

In pairs or triads, share your golfers list and then pray for one another.

Improving Your Serve

Objective: *One of the best ways to share the Gospel with people is to serve them. What are some practical ways to do this? How do we get started? These are the questions explored in this session.*

10-15
minutes

Discovery Activity

Stories of Kindness

Facilitator Instructions: Ask the group to share about a time when someone did something kind for them which was totally unexpected.

Debrief
Give everyone in the group a chance to share…the more stories, the better for this opening activity. After the stories have been shared ask the group to reflect together about these acts of kindness by asking:

Question #1: How did the act of kindness impact you personally? How did it make you feel?

Question #2: What makes kindness so powerful?

Question #3: Who comes to your mind when you think of kindness? How did or does that person embody kindness?

20-25
minutes

Learning Activity

Reaching Out With Kindness

Facilitator Instructions: Transition to the content on kindness with a reminder to the group about the concepts from the first session in "Natural Evangelism". The two key ideas to review relate to the image of a golf course and the faith stages a person works through in response to God's initiating love. Review what each of these people need by asking the group to restate the characteristics of each group below and how to best reach out to them. Highlight that this session is focused toward the People in the Tee Box.

> People in the Tee Box
> People in the Fairway
> People Approaching the Green
> People on the Putting Green

Bible Search on Kindness

Pair people up for this next activity. Ask everyone to look up the Bible passages provided and to record insights about kindness and compassion. Ask people to work quickly so that they have time to look up all of the passages. After 10 minutes, bring everyone back together to share their insights. Ask them to be brief and concise with their comments.

Passage	Insight About Kindness or Compassion
Romans 2:4	
Titus 3:4-5	
Zechariah 7:8-10	
Proverbs 3:3-4	
Hosea 10:12	
Isaiah 58:6-12	

Improving Your Serve

As we consider people who are far from God, whose "spiritual ball" is still in the tee box, our actions will speak louder than words. In fact, our words about God, Christianity, and the basic Gospel message will most likely fall on deaf ears until we have won the right to speak. Compassionate and thoughtful acts are sure-fire ways to melt the icy resistance of someone you know who's in the tee box area. The old adage, "kill 'em with kindness" is our mantra as we seek to "improve our serve."

In the book, *Irresistible Evangelism*, a working definition of kindness is suggested as "demonstrating God's love by offering to do humble acts of service, in Christ's name, with no strings attached" (91). The authors go on to say:

> We'll never shine brightly in the kingdom of God until we can sign up for activities that bring us no immediate, tangible, specific gain. We need to learn the lesson Jesus taught in Luke 6:35 about giving without expecting to get anything back, not even gratitude. The only reward we need is knowing that we're acting like sons of the Most High. The watching world will never be genuinely interested in our message as long as we come across as self-seeking promoters of our little piece of the kingdom. However, the world hungers for generosity in Christ's name when those expressing it don't care who gets the credit. If we don't take seriously the phrases in Christ's name and with no strings attached, we're just using a manipulative marketing strategy (94).

When we serve another, with no strings attached, we are operating in a way that is counter-cultural. Doing something for nothing is unheard of these days. A posture of a servant can easily be drowned out by the "me, my, and mine" slogans of Madison Avenue. But let's remember...it is the kindness of God that has drawn us into a saving relationship. Through His kindness, God has rescued us from the kingdom of darkness and pulled us out of the miry clay. Through His many acts of kindness in the New Testament, Jesus gives us a model of what it means to be kind.

Steve Sjogren, one of the co-authors of *Irresistible Evangelism*, shares a powerful personal story about acts of kindness. He was in the midst of recovering from a life threatening surgery-gone-bad. He wrote about his time in the hospital:

> I was at the lowest point of my life in every way- physically, emotionally, and spiritually; I desperately needed to give something away to get better. All I could think of that was available to me was Popsicles. So whenever visitors asked if there was anything they could do for me, I didn't even let them finish the sentence. "Have you got any pocket change?" I would ask. If they did, I'd have them roll me in my wheelchair down the hallway to the Popsicle machine. They would spring for a lap-full of the tasty treats, and then we would go up and down the hallways looking for patients to give them to. The only guideline: Only patients not on ventilators could get a Popsicle!

> I can't prove it, but I think I got better much faster by giving away all those Popsicles. It was my way of cooperating with God in my healing process. I had to get out of myself and get into principles that are much bigger than my circumstances- I got better and better as I gave away what I didn't even have in the first place.

Debrief
Question #1: What gets in the way of you performing acts of kindness?

Question #2: In what way are you personally challenged by what you just read?

15-20 minutes

Application Activity

Putting Feet to Your Service

Facilitator Instructions: Allow everyone to individually work through the worksheet entitled "Kindness Ideas". Have them mark ideas that would be possible acts of kindness that they could try out in the next week or before the next session. After everyone has scanned the list, have them share their ideas in small groups. Before you wrap-up the session, give everyone the challenge of doing something on the list before the next time you meet as a group. Close in prayer in the small groups.

Public Places
Soft Drink Giveaways
Newspapers
Vinyl Gloves
Umbrella Escorts
Windshield Washing
Coffee Giveaways
Restroom Cleaning
Urinal Screens
Restroom Deodorizer
Grocery Bag Loading
  Assistance
Bag Packing at Self-Serve
  Grocers
Grocery Cart Returns
Quarters Attached to Cards for
Phone Calls or Parking Meters
Donut Giveaway during
  Morning Traffic
Cookies
Lifesavers
Dollar Drop
Quarter Drop
Chewing Gum
Lollipops / Blow Pops
Small Bags of Taffy
Gourmet Chocolates (Truffles)
Bottled Water Giveaway
Flower Seeds
Freshen-up Packs - (mints &
  moist towelettes)

Sporting Events
Coffee Giveaways
Soft Drink Giveaways
Popcorn
Popsicles
Windshield Washing
Peanuts
Sunglasses (cheap ones!)
Hand Cleaning Towelettes
Freshen-up packs - (mints &
  moist towelettes)
Trash Pick Up
Bottled Water Giveaway
Glow in the Dark Necklaces

Downtown
Windshield Washing
Soft Drinks for Shoppers
Parking Meter Feeding
Umbrella Escorts

Business Window Washing
Toilet Cleaning
Cart Token for Shopping Carts
Employee Soft Drink
  Giveaway
Cookies
Cappuccino
Polaroids at Carriage Rides
Shoe Shines
Hand Cleaning Towelettes
Stamps in Front of Post Office
Seeds on Cars

Parks
Doggie Treats
Pet Festivals
Hot Dog Grilling
Helium Balloons for Kids
Polaroid Family Photos
Picnic
Ice Cream Coupons
Gatorade at Biking Trails
Pictionary in the Park
Flower Seed Packets
Face Painting
Doggie Dirt Cleanup
Doggie Wash
Golf Balls
Golf Tees
Golf Ball Cleaning
Pump-up Spray Water Bottles
Clowning
Bottled Water Giveaway

Automobiles
Car Wash
Windshield Washing
Check Oil and Fill
Single Mom's Oil Change
Washer Fluid Fill
Tire Pressure Check
Interior Vacuuming
Interior Window Cleaning
Bulb Replacement
Windshield Ice Scraping at
  Apartment Complexes
Windshield Ice Scrapers
Freeing Cars Stuck in Snow
Windshield Washing at Self-
  Serve Gas Stations
Buy Down Gas to Bargain
  Price

Car Drying at Car Washes
Hand Cleaning Towelettes at
  Gas Pumps

Roadsides & Traffic Lights
Parking Meter Feeding
Summer Car Washes
Coke Giveaways
Winter Car Washes/ Desalting
Popsicle Giveaways
Trash Pickup with "Kindness in
  Progress" Signs
Towelettes Giveaway on Side
  of the Road

College Campuses
Bike Fix-up
Pen and Pencil Giveaways
Post Cards and Stamps
Photocopying
Floppy Discs
Tutoring
Soft Drinks, Gatorade, and
  Lemonade at Class Sign-up
Dorm Room Cleaning
Drinks at Intramural Athletics
Drinks at Greek Events
Breakfast Pop Tarts
Test Essay Booklets
Exam Answer Sheets
Coffee and Tea during Late
  Night Study Sessions
Pizza on Move-In Day at
  Dorms
Quarter Drop
Long Distance Phone Cards
Ice Cream Coupons
Care Packages for Students
Gum, Blow Pops
Snacks (chips, crackers)

Malls & Shopping Centers
Christmas Gift Wrapping
Dollar Drop
Meal Purchasing at Food Court
Quarters in Coin Returns
Long Distance Phone Cards
Ice Cream Cone Coupons
Package Check-In
Childcare during Christmas
  Shopping
Coffee/Hot Chocolate Coupons

Holidays

Chocolate Hearts on Valentine's
Roses on Valentine's
Green Foiled Coins at St. Patrick's Day Parades
Easter Baskets for Businesses
Butterfly Cocoons for Easter
Easter Candy Giveaway
Flower Seeds for Spring
Mother's / Father's Day Carnation Giveaways
Independence Day Festival
Glow in the Dark Necklaces
July 4th Picnics
Independence Day Festival Giveaways: Blow Pops, Gum
Labor Day - School Supplies
Halloween - Reverse Trick or Treat (House to House to give them candy)
Thanksgiving - Door to Door Turkey
Door to Door Mums
Fall Candy Giveaway
Fall Leaf Raking
Christmas: Gift Wrap at Mall
Christmas: Giveaway Special
Caroling and Candy Canes
Door to Door Poinsettias
Scotch Tape Giveaway
Christmas Tree Giveaway
Snow Shoveling
Winter Survival Kit

High School & College Sports

Oranges for Football Practice
High School Sports Party
Watermelon after practice
Gatorade after a hard practice
Facilitate a community service project
Make hospital visits
Greet students & parents & help the freshmen move in
Baby-sit for the coaches
Physical therapy rehab
Care packages for finals week
Offer tutoring
Honor a team at your athletic meeting
Shovel manure
Go to lesser followed sports

Set up social settings
Make own Appreciation Day
Capture seasonal times with high touch ideas
Take a camera to games
Clean up after an event
Meet with freshmen for a coke
Organize surprise mini birthday parties
Give away peanuts/popcorn at sporting events
Offer to do videoing of a practice
Offer to keep stats
Free car washes for the athletic department

House to House

Fruit Giveaway
Sunday Morning Paper and Coffee Giveaways
Leaf Raking
Lawn Mowing
Grass Edging
Screen Cleaning
Rain Gutter Cleaning
Garbage Can Return from Curb
Food Delivery to Shut-Ins
Kitchen Cleanup
General Yard Cleanup
Door to Door Carnation
Tulip Bulbs
Potted Plant Giveaways
Flower Seed Packet Giveaways
Sidewalk Sweeping
Windshield Washing
Snow Removal from Walks and Drives
Window Washing
Minor House Repairs
General Interior Cleaning
Community Dinner
Doggie Yard Cleanup
Weed Spraying
Tree Limb Trimming
Light Bulb Replacement
Seal Blacktop Driveways
Fireplace Ash Removal
Radon Detectors
Carbon Monoxide Detectors
Smoke Detector Batteries
Fragrance Spraying
Dog Washing

Filter Change for AC / Heater
Garage Cleaning
Fireplace Kindling
Bark and Mulch for Yards
Salt for Snowy Driveways
House Number Painting on Curbs
Shopping Assistance for Shut-ins
Poinsettias at Christmas
Picnics at Independence Day
Easter Baskets

Miscellaneous

Steaks & Salmon for Firefighters
Gasoline for Your Neighbor
Cleaning Up at Food Courts
Toilet Seat Covers
Birthday Party Organizing
Pay Library Fines
Winter Survival Kit
Suntan Lotion
Surf Wax
Summer Survival Kit
"Biggie Size" Food Orders in Fast Food Drive Thru Lanes
Blood Pressure Screening
Mother's Day Carnation
Car Drying at Self-Serve Car Washes
Grocery Store Bag Packing
Free Bird Feeders and Refills to Convalescent Home Residents
Christmas Tree Collection
Christmas Tree Giveaway
Bait at Local Fishing Spots
Coffee at Bus or Subway Stops
Pay Laundromat Washer & Dryer
Memorial Service for Unchurched
Carnations to Cemetery Visitors
Easter Baskets
Pizza on Moving Day at Apartments
Move In Welcoming Party
Lawn Mower Tune-up
Time Change Reminder Flyer
Cocoons on Good Friday
Church Match Books
Scotch Tape at Christmas

Improve Your Serve Together

Objective: *It's one thing to serve people alone, but when you do it with others, the impact is multiplied. In this session, the group will discuss ways of serving together and how that can touch lives.*

10
minutes

Discovery Activity

Ice Breaker

Facilitator Instructions: Before jumping into the session, ask everyone to report about how things went with the kindness ideas from the last module. Celebrate any sense of advancement or steps taken in the right direction!

After the initial check-in, transition to the opening sharing question: Can you share about a time when you were part of a group that made a difference in other people's lives? What was the experience like for you personally, for the group, and for the lives you touched?

Once a number of people have shared, ask the group to reflect on the stories by asking: What are some of the benefits of working together when you are trying to extend love to others?

Video Clip: Sister Act

Facilitator Instructions: (The scene starts at 58:28 and ends at 1:03:15.) (If your local video rental store does not carry this movie, you can order it online on www.Amazon.com or similar websites.) If you think your group will not be offended, you could start the clip a little earlier at 53:51. Preview it first to see if you think there is any offensive language in the interaction between Whoopi Goldberg and the Reverend Mother after the performance…the choir music is quite fun! Set up the scene with the following description: Whoopi Goldberg plays a Las Vegas singer who is on the run from her gangster boyfriend. The police stash her away in a Catholic Convent where Whoopi has just been given the charge of developing the choir. Watch what happens in this interaction between the "street-smart" Whoopi and the ultra-conservative Reverend Mother.

Debrief
Question #1: How would you describe the values of Whoopi, the Reverend Mother, and the Nuns?

Question #2: What dynamics did you notice unfolding in the scene as the nuns "took to the streets?" What did you observe as the nuns worked together?

Question #3: How are you personally challenged by what you saw in this scene?

Learning Activity

Improving Your Serve (Together!)

Facilitator Instructions: Spend time in the book of Nehemiah to underscore what happens when a group of people put their minds toward "improving their serve together!" Allow everyone time to look up each of the passages on their own first and then discuss each passage individually. There is a progression as the book of Nehemiah unfolds. Try to highlight the dynamics of a group of people going after the project together. Instruct the group: Look through these passages and reflect on how vision for working together emerged and became a reality in the life of Nehemiah and those around him.

The book of Nehemiah continues the history of the Jews upon their return from exile in Babylon. Nehemiah was commissioned to go to Jerusalem to lead the people in repairing the protective walls around the city. Nehemiah was a spiritual leader who led with vision and passion.

Passage	Insights about Improving Your Serve (Together!)
Neh. 1:1-4	
Neh. 1:11-2:5	
Neh. 2:11-13	
Neh. 2:17-18	
Neh. 2:19-20, 4:1-3	
Neh. 4:12-21	
Neh. 6:15-16	

Facilitator Instructions: After you have had time to discuss Nehemiah, ask everyone to read the short article "Improving your Serve (Together!)".

Improving Your Serve (Together!)

The book of Nehemiah reminds us that a group can accomplish great things for the Kingdom. It started with a legitimate need and a compassionate response. Once Nehemiah heard about the broken walls in Jerusalem, his heart was moved. Eventually he was able to motivate others to join him in the quest to rebuild the protective walls around the city.

In the book, *Irresistible Evangelism,* several helpful principles regarding serving together are discussed (pages 97-105). Let's consider a few of those principles for a moment…

Keep it Simple: Acts of kindness don't have to be elaborate, expensive, or complicated to do. With some creativity and brainstorming there are a number of ways to extend love to others that are easy to pull off. In the initial stages of improving your serve, the simpler the better.

Low Risk, High Grace: When deciding on a project, choose something which is low risk for you and your partners. Handing soft drinks out at a community soccer match might be considered high risk for some people. But putting a packet of flower seeds in mailboxes could be more comfortable. But be forewarned…acts of kindness are contagious. Once you start blessing people with no strings attached it can become addictive. So get the ball rolling and watch what opportunities the Lord lays on your heart.

It's a Process: Remember, people don't care what we know until they know that we care about them as individuals. Performing acts of kindness and compassion is one way to demonstrate care that moves folks down the fairway. It's a process for us, too! Many of us need to develop our under-used serving muscles. We're not used to extending kindness to others with no strings attached.

Have Fun! Improving your serve together can and should be outrageously fun. Blessing others can bring tremendous enjoyment. What better way to speak to our culture today than by having a great time through service? That's the kind of Christianity that is winsome and attractive in a culture that has lost its way.

Just do it…like Now! The old adage, "There's no day like today!" So, go on…get out there and just do it. Don't procrastinate. Take some of the "Improving Your Serve" ideas and just start lovin' on some folks. Team up with some people you know and go make somebody's day.

Debrief
Question #1: What idea or principle stands out to you from this article?

Question #2: What are you personally challenged by in the article?

Application Activity

Taking it to the Streets

Facilitator Instructions: Give some advance thought as to how you would like to handle this final activity. It could be a whole group activity or done in smaller teams. The goal is to put a simple plan of action together from the Improving Your Serve Together Ideas. Many ideas are the same as the previous session's list. Give everyone the freedom to generate an idea that's not on the list. Review the article below for a real life example. If you have time at the end of the session, ask the group to report in on what they intend to do. Close in prayer in groups or in the large group.

OIL CHANGES CHANGE LIVES

Auto outreach is 'touching' the community

The sign read "Free Oil Change, Because Jesus Changed Us." As cars and truck passed, drivers could not miss it.

Nor could they miss the fact that the parking lot of the church was full with cars lined up to enter one of the three oil-changing bays.

A church leader greeted people as they pulled into the parking lot. He was met with stares of disbelief, then big smiles of gratitude as they steered SUVs, pickup trucks and four-door sedans onto steel ramps for a free oil and filter change, along with a 14-point check of fluids, tires and lights.

One of the pastors in the church explains why they do this: "We want the community to know we're here, so we do something different every week. Last week, we had a free carwash. And we've helped clean up the nature trail at a local school. And one week, we went into the subdivisions and prayed over each of the houses."

One leader explained, "It's something everyone needs. We're hoping some single mothers might take advantage of it, but also anyone else who needs one. Sometimes you're just so busy, you can't find time for one."

As you walk past the cars in line, all kinds of stories are represented. One single mom confessed, "My car is two-months overdue for an oil change. This is awesome." An elderly lady who lives near the church explained, "I've lived in this neighborhood for 30 years, but I never paid attention to them until they started giving to the community like this." An unemployed father of eight who had just moved to the area was overwhelmed with gratitude.

Interestingly, those serving included a wide range of people. Teenagers were working alongside retirees, both stating that they love to invest in the community. One high school student stated, "I get to do what I love doing—work on cars—and we get to have fun serving others."

While the oil changing occurred outside, a team of volunteers worked inside, writing short letters to various people who had visited the church. They want to make it clear that God makes a tangible difference in our real lives. Everyone in the church knows that they are called to make a difference in the community in a physical way.

Improving Your Serve Together Ideas

- ❏ Soft Drink Giveaway
- ❏ Newspapers
- ❏ Windshield Washing
- ❏ Coffee Giveaway
- ❏ Restroom Cleaning
- ❏ Grocery Bag Loading Assistance
- ❏ Grocery Cart Returns
- ❏ Donut Giveaway during Morning Traffic
- ❏ Cookies
- ❏ Bottled Water Giveaway
- ❏ Flower Seeds
- ❏ Popcorn
- ❏ Popsicles
- ❏ Windshield Washing
- ❏ Hand Cleaning Towelettes
- ❏ Trash Pick Up
- ❏ Glow in the Dark Necklace Giveaway
- ❏ Parking Meter Feeding
- ❏ Hot Dog Grilling
- ❏ Helium Balloons for Kids
- ❏ Polaroid Family Photos
- ❏ Picnic
- ❏ Ice Cream Coupons
- ❏ Gatorade at Biking Trails
- ❏ Face Painting
- ❏ Doggie Dirt Cleanup
- ❏ Doggie Wash
- ❏ Clowning
- ❏ Single Mom's Oil Change
- ❏ Summer Car Washes
- ❏ Popsicle Giveaway
- ❏ Trash Pickup with "Kindness in Progress" Signs
- ❏ Tutoring
- ❏ Drinks at Athletic Events
- ❏ Care Packages for Students
- ❏ Snacks (chips, crackers)
- ❏ Christmas Gift Wrapping
- ❏ Childcare
- ❏ Oranges for High School Practice
- ❏ High School Sports Party
- ❏ Facilitate Community Service Project
- ❏ Make Hospital Visits
- ❏ Greet Students and Parents and Help the Freshmen Move In
- ❏ Baby-sit for Coaches
- ❏ Take a Camera to Practice/ Games
- ❏ Clean Up after a Sporting Event
- ❏ Give Away Peanuts/Popcorn at Sporting Events
- ❏ Offer To Do Videoing of a Team's Practice
- ❏ Fruit Giveaway
- ❏ Sunday Morning Paper and Coffee Giveaways
- ❏ Leaf Raking
- ❏ Lawn Mowing
- ❏ Grass Edging
- ❏ Screen Cleaning
- ❏ Rain Gutter Cleaning
- ❏ Garbage Can Return from the Curb
- ❏ Food Delivery to Shut-Ins
- ❏ General Yard Cleanup
- ❏ Door to Door Carnation Giveaway
- ❏ Tulip Bulbs
- ❏ Potted Plant Giveaway
- ❏ Sidewalk Sweeping
- ❏ Minor House Repairs
- ❏ Community Dinner
- ❏ Weed Spraying
- ❏ Tree Limb Trimming
- ❏ Garage Cleaning
- ❏ Bark and Mulch for Yards
- ❏ House Number Painting on Curbs
- ❏ Steaks and Salmon for Firefighters
- ❏ Free Bird Feeders and Refills to Convalescent Home Residents
- ❏ Move In Welcoming Party

Friendship Through Listening

Objective: *Listening demonstrates that we care for others. These exercises will help group members develop listening skills so that we can truly understand others' needs.*

15
minutes

Discovery Activity

Back-to-Back Drawing Debrief

Facilitator Instructions:
Round #1
Pair participants for this exercise. Have partners sit back to back. One partner has a simple picture (Choose four or five different simple pictures from a magazine.). The other partner is given a blank piece of paper with which to draw on. Partner #1 (holding the picture): "You have 3-4 minutes to describe your picture to your partner." Partner #2 (with blank paper): "Your job is to try and reproduce your partner's picture from the verbal cues he or she gives you. You are not allowed to ask any questions or give your partner any verbal feedback. You are to quietly draw your picture."

Round #2
Simply reverse roles. Make sure to hand out two different pictures to the pairings so that they are drawing a fresh picture and one that they have not heard other groups trying to draw. Same ground rules for the pairings as there were from Round #1.

Question #1: What was it like being the clue giver?

Question #2: What was it like being the one drawing?

Question #3: In what ways does this exercise illustrate effective communication?

Question #4: What was it like for you personally when you felt really listened to?

15
minutes

Learning Activity

Friendship Through Listening

Facilitator Instructions: Ask people to read the enclosed article. Encourage them to underline and mark principles that stand out.

> My dear brothers, take note of this: Everyone should be quick to listen, slow to speak, and slow to become angry, for man's anger does not bring about the righteous life that God desires. —James 1:19-20

It's been said that God gave us two ears and one mouth for a reason. One of the gifts that we give to those that we listen to is focused attention through our listening. All of us long to have someone who is interested in our circumstances, our challenges, and our triumphs. Building friendships with unbelievers requires our attentive listening. People all around you have a hunger to be heard... by you!

Becoming a focused listener takes practice though. It's an art that takes work and effort on our part. One of the primary issues that we must wrestle with is our propensity to listen autobiographically. Stephen Covey, in his book *The 7 Habits of Highly Effective People*, talks about four ways that we allow autobiographical listening to get in the way of true listening.

First, we often evaluate what others are saying. We begin wondering if we agree or disagree with the other person's perspective. Are they right or wrong? Are their values in-line with what I think they should be or not? Next, if we're not careful we will probe the person we are listening to from our own frame of reference. Did they handle this the way that I handled it in the past? Did this impact them the way it impacted me?

Third, we can be guilty of interpreting the other person's circumstances based on our own motives and behavior. We try to figure people out and explain their motives and behavior through what we would do or what motivates us. We project ourselves into their story.

And finally, we then move to giving advice from what we have found helpful from our past experiences. We start fixing the other person from what has worked for us. We think, "Surely what has worked for me will work for you."

When we listen autobiographically, we rob the other person of an opportunity to be listened to without obstructive filters. Our past, our motives, our emotions are not what people need from us. They need someone who will get himself out of the way, open up his ears, and give his full undivided attention. Cultivating a friendship means that we understand the principle, "When we're talking, we're not listening."

Most of us will need to tame our desire to listen autobiographically at different times. However, there are three core listening skills that will go a long way toward taming "me-centered" listening. Those three skills are:

(1) Clarifying,
(2) Word Pictures, and
(3) Acknowledging.

Clarifying

One of the best ways to demonstrate that you're listening is to mirror back what you hear them saying. Phrases that clarify sound like:

"Is this what I hear you saying?"
"I sense that this is what you are saying..."
"It feels to me like you are describing... Is that accurate?"
"Let me reflect back to you what I'm hearing..."

Clarifying demonstrates that you are listening for emotional texture and factual connections. It helps the other person know that you are tracking with them and that you understand how they view things.

Word Pictures

Word Pictures tap into the right side of the brain and help the person to access feelings. Creating word pictures is a skill that takes practice and demonstrates effective listening. For example:

> For someone who is confused you might say… "it sounds like you are in a fog."

> For someone who is irritated you might say… "it feels like nails going down a chalk board."

> For someone entering a time of risk… "you're about to get up on a big wave."

> For someone in a chaotic work environment… "it sounds like a cyclone."

Acknowledging

When we acknowledge, we are communicating that we are able to "read between the lines" of what the other person is saying. Acknowledging is a powerful way to demonstrate that you've been listening on more than one level. It is a way to validate and to affirm the person for what you see in them. It's more about who they are than it is about what they are doing. Some acknowledging comments would be:

> "It sounds like this has been a very fulfilling time for you."
> "It feels like you are making significant progress."
> "I hear a sense of disappointment from you when you talk about this setback."
> "That took a tremendous amount of courage on your part."
> "You are showing significant commitment to make this change in your life … Way to go!"

Debrief

Question #1: How do you fall into the trap of autobiographical listening?

Question #2: Which of the four autobiographical listening tracks do you find yourself taking when listening to others?

Question #3: What stands out to you about the three listening skills of Clarifying, Word Pictures, and Acknowledging?

Application Activity

Case Study

Facilitator Instructions: Have everyone read the case study and then break up into triads to work through the case study interaction exercises. After 10 minutes, bring everyone back together for a discussion on the case study. Ask the groups to report about the various kinds of listening responses they recorded.

A neighbor whom you have befriended had this to say in a recent conversation:

> "I'm really disappointed with the experience that my son is having in Little League. We weren't sure if we should let him go up to the upper division this year. Now we know we made a mistake. I feel so bad for him. He gets to bat once a game and play two innings in right field. On top of that, the coach keeps yelling at Tommy, which has only made things worse. My husband would like to strangle the coach! I mean, where are the good old days, when youth sports used to be fun and not so competitive? At this point, my son is telling us that he doesn't want to play baseball anymore. Can you imagine that? Baseball used to be so fun for him. He would play endlessly in the neighborhood. And now, to have it all come to such an abrupt stop because of one lousy coach. It's soooo frustrating... and I feel partially to blame because he could have played in a lower division this year and we probably would have avoided all of this!"

Round #1: Autobiographical Listening Missteps
If you were listening to this neighbor in the above case study, what would be some examples of autobiographical listening on your part? In other words, pretend that you have an opportunity to listen to this frustrated mother. What would be some of the autobiographical missteps?

Evaluating:

Probing:

Advising:

Interpreting:

Round #2: <u>Core Listening Skills</u>
If you were the listener in the above case study, what would be some examples of three core listening skills? In other words, pretend that you have an opportunity to respond to this neighbor. How would you do it through Clarifying, Word Pictures, and Acknowledging?

Clarifying:

Word Pictures:

Acknowledging:

20 minutes

Listening Practice

Facilitator Instructions: Break the room up into partners for some real life listening practice. "You'll each have seven minutes to listen to one another. When you are the person sharing, determine an area of your life that you would like to talk about. It could be a problem, a challenge, an opportunity, or a circumstance you find yourself in. When you are listening, try to talk as little as possible. Try to practice the three core skills of Clarifying, Word Pictures, and Acknowledging."

5-10 minutes

Wrap-Up

Debrief: Bring the group together for a time to debrief and celebrate the learning by asking:

Question #1: How was it for you to practice the listening skills?

Question #2: What was it like being on the receiving end of someone listening to you?

Question #3: What is a new insight you've gained through this module?

Question #4: What is one way that you can improve as a listener?

In pairs or triads, have each person identify an unbeliever that they would like to practice listening with this coming week. Close by praying for those conversations.

Friendship Through Curiosity

Objective: *When we ask others good questions, we open doors for honest conversation. And honest conversations lead to trust-filled friendships. The exercises in this session will equip the group to ask great questions.*

10-15
minutes

Discovery Activity

The Question Game

Facilitator Instructions: Break the room up into teams of 3-5 people for a group competition game. The assignment for each team is to come up with as many questions as possible that could be used in getting to know someone better.

For example, you could ask: "What aspect of your work do you enjoy the most these days?" or "What did you like most about the area where you grew up?"

Let the group know that prizes (make sure you get some candy before the workshop) will be awarded in the following categories:

Category #1: Most thought-provoking question
Category #2: Group with the most questions

Each group has three minutes to generate their questions. All questions need to be recorded on paper. The Facilitator is the final judge for which group wins the prize in each category.

Debrief:
After the presentations and awards have been given out, gather everyone back together in a large group and discuss together this question: What happens inside of you when someone asks a great question?

10-15
minutes

Learning Activity

Friendships Through Curiosity

Curiosity killed the cat or so the saying goes. But curiosity is a basic building block for any relationship. Curious people are pretty rare these days though. In a time-poor, fast-paced culture, who has the time to be curious? Most of us live life with this as our motto: "Just give me the facts, please, and then I can move about my business."

However, pausing enough to slow down and show genuine, authentic interest in the life of an unbeliever is powerful. Earlier, in the *Natural Evangelism* series, we compared sharing the love and message of Christ to the game of golf. Our friends are at different places on their way to God. Some are just getting starting in "the tee box," while others are moving down the fairway in their journey toward God. Demonstrating curiosity enables us to make significant emotional deposits, no matter where our unbelieving friends are.

Listen to what a few authors have to say about curiosity:

Authentic curiosity is also a powerful builder of relationships…Imagine yourself at a dinner party seated next to a stranger who seems infinitely curious about you: your life, your work, your interests, what makes you tick, what ticks you off. This kind of curiosity is not only flattering but encouraging. It allows you to reveal a lot of yourself in an unchallenged way, and so you build a connection effortlessly.
(*Co-Active Coaching* by Whitworth, Kimsey-House, and Sandahl, 66)

So, what will it take for you to become a more curious person? Here are a few things to consider:

Principle #1: Jesus was a curious person.
Jesus loved to ask questions and to engage in open–ended conversations with people He met. He engaged the woman at the well (John 4:1-26), the disciples (John 1:43-51), the prostitutes (Matt. 9:9-12), and the lame (Matt. 8:1-4) with authenticity that indicated He was truly interested in the other person. The world screams, "It's all about me!" while Jesus demonstrated over and over again that, "It's all about others!" He was quick to identify the needs, concerns, and passions of those He touched. To be curious means we need to get out of ourselves and our own worlds. It means we need to look at life from someone else's vantage point by simply being curious.

Principle #2: Listening and curiosity are cousins.
When we listen well we have the opportunity to keep a conversation going. In *Irresistible Evangelism* the authors liken conversations to tennis matches. A good conversation goes back and forth on both sides of the net. When we show that we are listening and hit the ball back over the net we keep a conversation going. Which leads to the third principle…

Principle #3: Being curious means asking questions.
Asking questions that get people talking about their lives is a critical part of cultivating a friendship. Learning to ask questions that open people up is something that anyone can learn to do with a little practice. There are a few clear characteristics of a great question. The list below underscores a few of the qualities we should strive for when framing a question. A good question should:

- be easily understood
- not be complex
- require thought
- encourage self-disclosure
- not allow for one word answers

Using open-ended questions that draw out the person is a skill that takes practice and the discipline of listening rather than talking. We must expand our capacity to ask the "second question." That is to say, as we listen actively, we need to consider the next question we can ask that will keep the "tennis match" going. The "second question" is often the question that will yield the greatest insight and connection with another person.

Debrief

Question #1: What stands out to you in this article?

Question #2: What is the most challenging part of asking questions for you?

Question #3: What are some of the varied benefits of asking questions?

Question #4: What are some ways Jesus practiced curiosity?

15 minutes

Application Activity

Questions You Could Ask

Facilitator Instructions: Have everyone partner up and tell them to develop questions that you could ask another person with the various categories provided below. Work hard at creating curious and open-ended questions! After everyone has had 5-7 minutes to generate some questions, bring the group back together to cross-pollinate and share what they've come up with.

Category	Questions You Could Ask
Someone just moved into the neighborhood	
Hobbies/free time	
Career	
Family background	
Family events	
Religious background	
Movies	
Current events	
Vacation	
Someone experiencing change	

Application Activity

Being Curious Practice

Facilitator Instructions: Mix up the room for this activity so that people are paired with someone different. Instructions for the group: "This is a practice session highlighting the skill of listening, being curious, and asking questions. That's all you get to do…no commenting, no advice giving, no talking about yourself. This is completely about being curious about the other person! This is a time to dig deeper and to practice the skill of asking the 'second question.'"

• One person gets to talk and share about any topic (work, home, background, hobbies, etc.).

• One person listens and asks questions that draw the other person out further.

"You have 7 minutes for your conversation. At the end of 7 minutes, I'll have you give a little feedback to your partner and then we will switch roles."

Debrief
After all of the conversations have concluded, ask the group to comment on the whole experience by responding to:

Question #1: What was it like to be listened to?

Question #2: What was it like to stay in a curious posture?

Wrap-Up

In triads, close out the session by asking everyone to respond to these two questions:

Question #1: The major insight I've gained from this training module is....

Question #2: What unbelieving friend will I practice being more curious with in the next week?

After sharing, close in prayer in the groupings, focusing on the future conversations folks are hoping to have.

Natural Sharing

Objective: *Telling your story of how you began your journey with Jesus is a conversational way of sharing the Gospel. In this session, we will learn the steps for sharing our stories.*

20
minutes

Discovery Activity

Symbol Timeline

Facilitator Instructions: Give everyone 6-8 minutes to draw pictures called a "symbol timeline" of the major people, events, and circumstances that have shaped who they are from birth to today. Encourage everyone to use pictures only. After the allotted time ask people to share their symbol timeline with someone that they would like to get to know better. Each person gets 5 minutes to share.

A symbol timeline gives you a big picture of God's shaping of your life by using a series of symbols that depict your journey. It is simply a symbolic way to tell your story, starting from birth on the left, up to the present on the right. The symbols could contain positive and negative experiences. Use any symbols you'd like to tell the story of your life.

Examples of possible symbols:

> Close family relationships
> Conversion to Christ
> Sports - Soccer Team
> Graduation, etc.

Create your own symbols and personal symbol timeline below. Focus on people, circumstances, and events that have shaped your life.

This is not an art contest, have fun!

My Symbol Timeline

Debrief
What are some of the reasons that we like to share and listen to stories? In other words, what makes stories so powerful?

*Points you'll want to make in addition are:

> - stories touch our emotions
> - stories help us connect with another person
> - stories are credible because they're from our own lives

<u>Key point</u>: God has done very unique things in our lives. Some very powerful stories reside in each one of us. Our story with God can and needs to be shared with those who need to find God.

Learning Activity

10 minutes

Writing Your Own Story

One of the most effective ways of sharing our faith is by telling a story about our own journey with God. Jesus said to his disciples after the resurrection,

> You will be my witnesses in Jerusalem, and in all Judea and Samaria, and to the ends of the earth. —Acts 1:8

A witness is someone who tells his or her story or first-hand experience for those who have not shared in that experience. Stories are powerful! Today, let's take a look at the steps involved in writing a personal story about how God has been at work in your life recently or in the past. It could be something from your symbol timeline or something else that comes to mind. The point is, one of the ways we can weave God into our friendships with unbelievers is through the use of personal stories of change and growth.

Facilitator Instructions:
1. Briefly take the group through the five steps of writing their own story which are listed on the following pages.

2. Then turn everyone loose to work on their own story. Let them know that they have 10 minutes to work on their draft. Pay close attention to folks who have been Christians from early childhood. Walk around and help them write their story from the vantage point of a time when God intervened in their life. Help them find a "grace story" that a non-believer would be able to relate to.

3. After everyone has worked on their draft, have them get into pairs or triads depending on how much time you have available. Triads will take a little bit longer but is a better experience overall. Give each person 5 minutes to share their story with their partner(s). Ask the listeners to give 2 minutes of feedback on their story...

- What went well?
- Was anything unclear?
- Any ways to polish their story for more impact?

4. Close out the session back in pairs/triads. Have everyone share the name of a non-Christian that they would like to share their story with in the next week (or your own predetermined period of time). Encourage people to create the opportunity by saying something like this: "I'm taking a class (or course) at my church and one of my assignments this week is to share a story with a friend about my life with God. Would you mind if I grabbed 10 minutes (now) or sometime this week to tell you a little bit about my life? I promise...no strings attached or Bible thumping!"

Challenge everyone to make a commitment to share their story. End with prayer in the sharing pairs or triads. Pray by name for those that will be shared with.

30 minutes

Application Activity

Steps to Writing Your Story

Step #1   Identify a time when God worked in your life.

Step #2   What were the circumstances?

Step #3   How I realized I needed Christ to help me.

Step #4   How I committed my life to Christ.

Step #5   The difference it has made in my life.

Step #1 Identify a time when God worked in your life.
Looking at the list of Life and Heart Themes, check the boxes where you have experienced God meeting your need.

Life and Heart Themes

❑ Worries/Anxiety . . . . Inner Peace
❑ Guilt/Shame. . . . . Forgiveness
❑ Anger/Temper . . . . Patience and love
❑ Emptiness/Lack of Purpose. . . Purpose in life
❑ Grief. Comfort and joy

- ❑ Stress/Burnout . . . . Power for living
- ❑ Low Self-Esteem . . . . Significance to God
- ❑ Poor Health . . . . Strength to go on
- ❑ Disappointment . . . . Trust in His good plans
- ❑ Insecurity . . . . Confidence and security
- ❑ Regrets . . . . A second chance at life
- ❑ Discontent/Always Busy . . . . . Contentment and peace
- ❑ Fears . . . . Faith to face my fears
- ❑ Loneliness . . . . He's always with me
- ❑ Addictions/Habits . . . . Power to change
- ❑ Self-Centeredness . . . . Love for other people
- ❑ Despair/Depression . . . . Hope
- ❑ Cheap Thrills . . . . Real, lasting happiness
- ❑ Boredom with My Life . . . . Adventure with God
- ❑ Fear of Death . . . . Assurance of heaven
- ❑ "Something Was Missing" . . . . Sense of fulfillment
- ❑ Bitterness & Resentment . . . . . Freedom from my past
- ❑ Pain of Rejection . . . . God's unconditional love
- ❑ Marriage Problems . . . . Changes in my marriage
- ❑ Financial Problems . . . . Changes in my finances
- ❑ Business Problems . . . . Changes in my business

Step #2 What my life was like distant from Christ?
What substitute, if any, for God did you use to find meaning in your life? (sports/fitness, success at work, marriage, sex, making money, drugs/alcohol, having fun, entertainment, popularity, hobbies)
*If you've been a believer since early childhood, then reflect on this question: "What are some difficulties or challenges that God has helped you face that could serve as a connecting point, as a window of grace, with a non-believer?"

Step #3 How I realized I needed Christ to help me.
How did God get your attention?
What motivated you?
What needs, hurts or problems added to your realization that you needed Jesus' help?
What did you try on your own that didn't work?

Step #4 How I was drawn near to Christ.
How did you ask God to help you?
How did you ask God to get involved?
What did He do?
What Bible passage was especially meaningful to you at this time?

Step #5 The difference Jesus has made in my life.
What benefits have you experienced or felt?
What problems have been resolved?
How has Jesus helped you change for the better?
How has it helped your relationships?

5-10 minutes

Wrap-Up

Facilitator Instructions: If it is appropriate, take some time to highlight two things before you close out the *Natural Evangelism* series:

1. Ask volunteers to share personal highlights from the series. How did they grow and what were some of their major learnings?

2. In pairs or triads, have each person identify an unbeliever that they would like to practice listening with this coming week. Close by praying for those conversations.